A Fantastic Trip

by Narinder Dhami

illustrated by Erin Brown

It was a hot morning. Roopa and Hardeep were going to the coast.

Roopa wanted to fish in the rock pools.
Hardeep wanted to sail his boat.

"We cannot go to the coast now," said Mum. "Dad is feeling ill."

Roopa and Hardeep were very disappointed.

"It's not fair!" Hardeep howled.

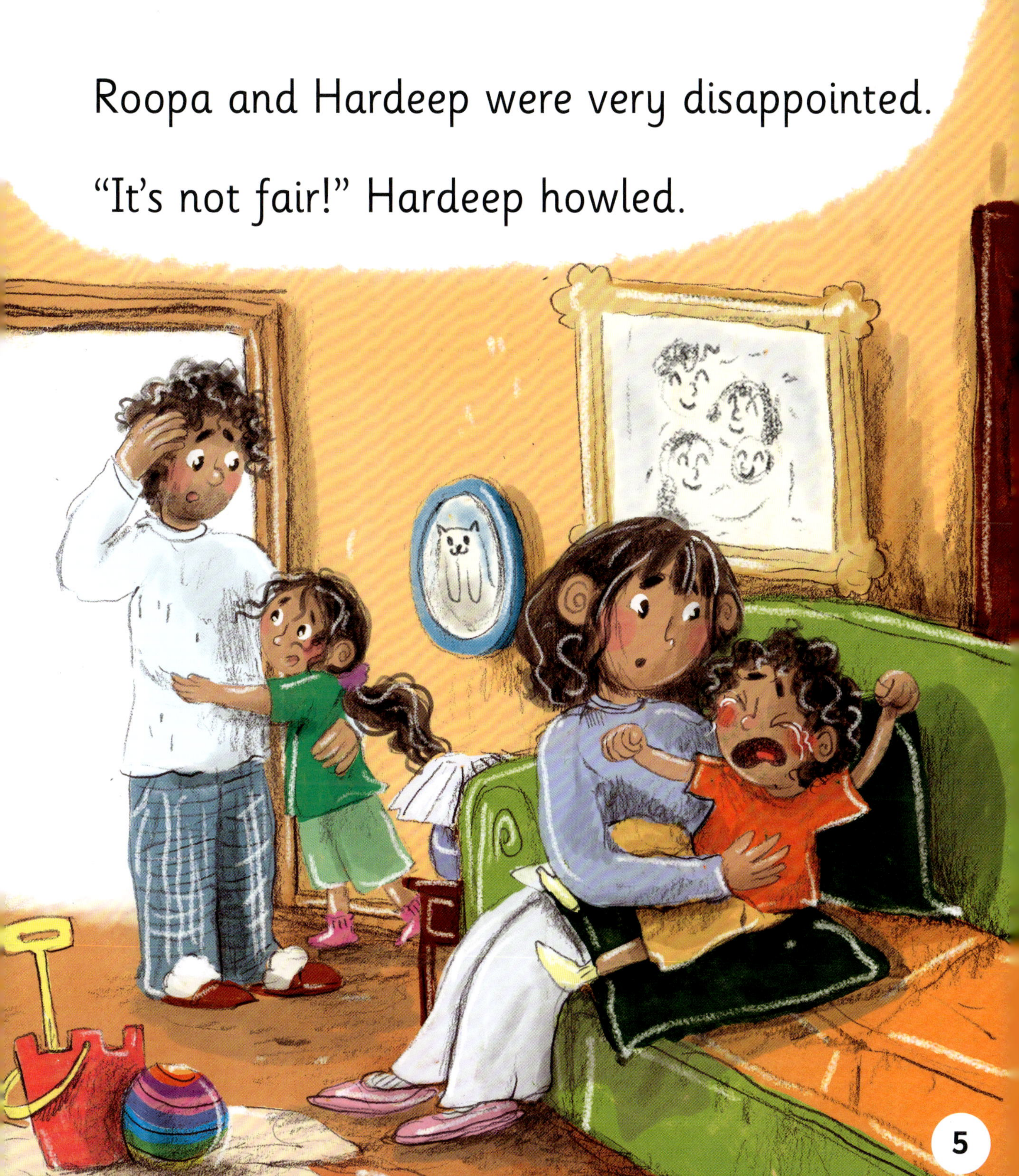

"We can still go to the coast," Roopa said. "Wait and see!"

Roopa turned the tap on. Mum started filling the pool.

The pool filled up with cool water. Then Roopa and Mum cleared out the sand pit.

They laid the sand near the pool. Then they got the deckchairs out.

The children rushed to get their things.

Roopa and Hardeep splashed in the water.

"Look out for the shark!" Hardeep yelled.

They dug a fort in the sand. It had tall towers and a moat.

Then Mum laid out a picnic.

Dad joined them. He was feeling a lot better.

We had a fantastic
trip to the coast!

Look Back

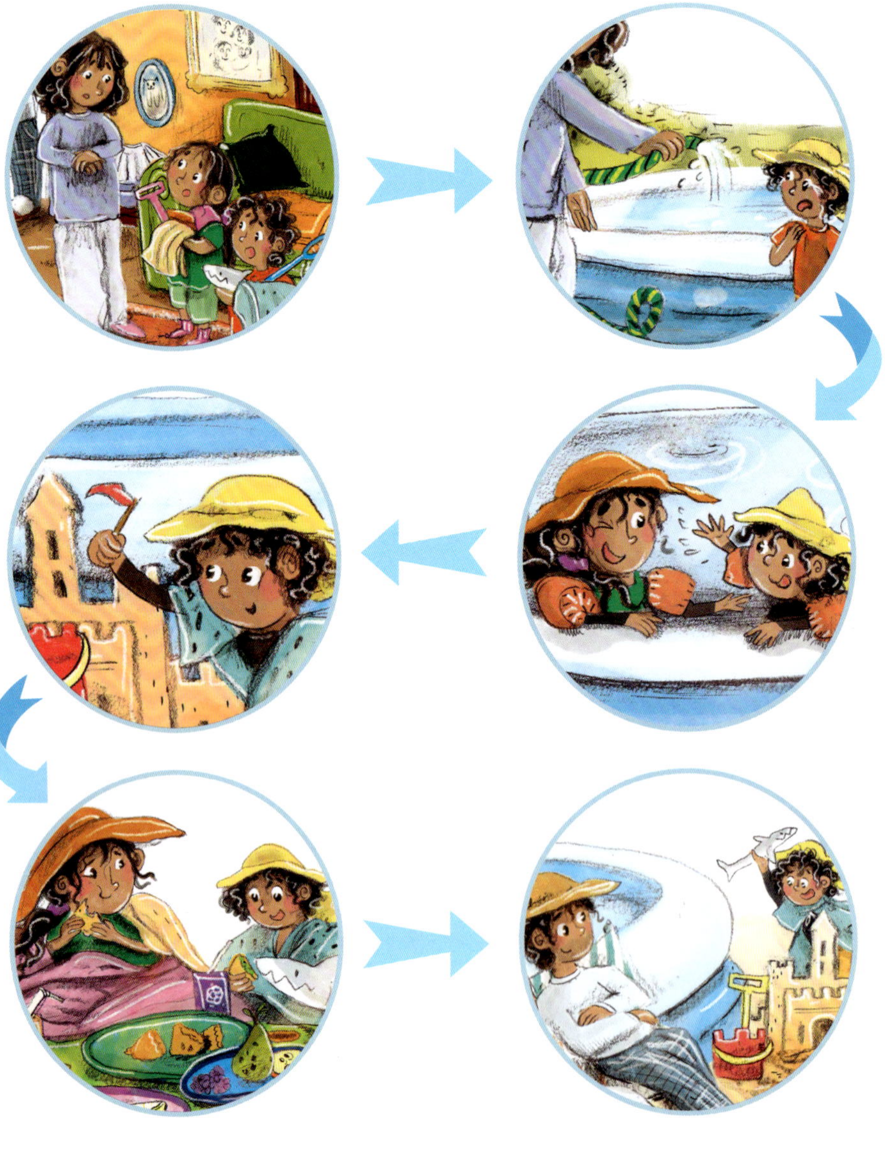

Encourage students to use the pictures to retell the story.